D0503635

WORLD WINDOWS

The City and the Country

HEINLE CENGAGE Learning™

Y|S|G A YBM COMPANY Young & Son Global, Inc.

Do you live in the city or the country?

Contents

Vocabulary	4	Where People Work	12
The City and the Country	6	Summary	14
Where People Live	8	Song	15
How People Travel	10	Index	16

Vocabulary
the city
subway
indoors

outdoors
tractor
the country

The City and the Country

People live in the city or in the country. There are many streets and buildings in the city.

The country is different.
There are many fields and trees in the country.

Where People Live

In the city, people live in houses or apartment buildings. People live close together.

In the country, people live in houses and on farms.

People live far apart from each other.

How People Travel

People in the city drive cars. They also take taxis and the subway.

The subway train travels underground.

People in the country drive cars, too.

They also drive tractors and trucks.

These children are riding in a tractor.

Where People Work

In the city, people work in offices and use computers.
They work indoors.

Office workers use computers.

On a farm, people raise animals and grow their own vegetables. They work outdoors.

This farmer is holding some carrots.

Summary

How are the city and the country different?

the city	the country

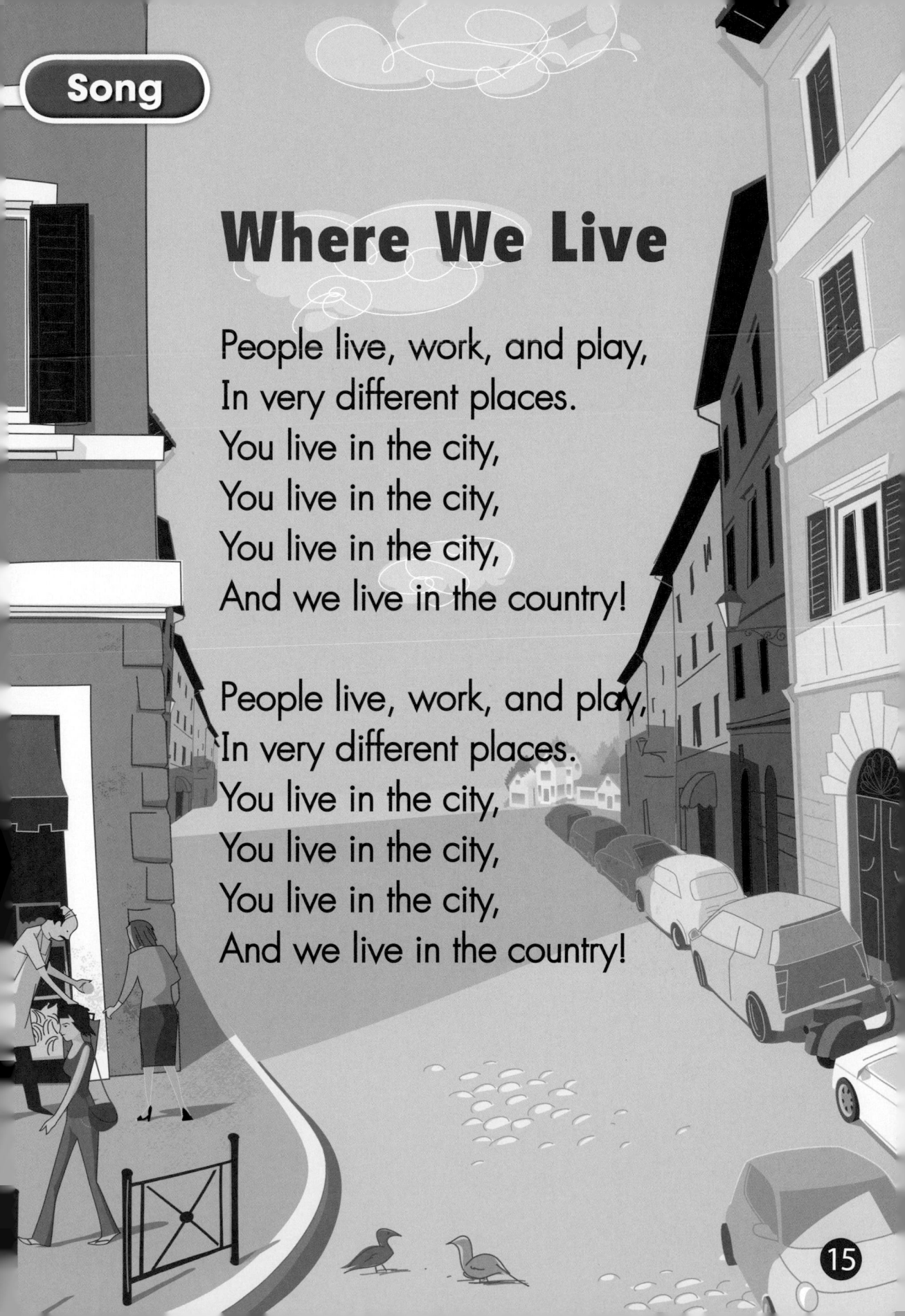

Song

Where We Live

People live, work, and play,
In very different places.
You live in the city,
You live in the city,
You live in the city,
And we live in the country!

People live, work, and play,
In very different places.
You live in the city,
You live in the city,
You live in the city,
And we live in the country!

Index

apartment buildings, 8

cars, 10–11

drive, 10–11

houses, 8–9

indoors, 12

live, 6, 8–9

offices, 12

outdoors, 13

subway, 10

taxis, 10

the city, 6, 8, 10, 12

the country, 6–7, 9, 11

tractors, 11

trucks, 11

work, 12–13